IN SHORT

IN SHORT

Private Notes of a Psychoanalyst

Salman Akhtar

First published in 2024 by
Karnac Books Limited
62 Bucknell Road
Bicester
Oxfordshire OX26 2DS

Copyright © 2024 by Salman Akhtar

The right of Salman Akhtar to be identified as the author of this work has been asserted in accordance with §§ 77 and 78 of the Copyright Design and Patents Act 1988.

All rights reserved. No part of this publication may be reproduced, stored in a retrieval system, or transmitted, in any form or by any means, electronic, mechanical, photocopying, recording, or otherwise, without the prior written permission of the publisher.

British Library Cataloguing in Publication Data

A C.I.P. for this book is available from the British Library

ISBN-13: 978-1-80013-246-7

Typeset by Medlar Publishing Solutions Pvt Ltd, India

www.firingthemind.com

To

My wise, creative, and good-hearted daughter

NISHAT AKHTAR

Contents

Introduction   *xv*

Part I: Preparation

  1. Reading Freud   3
  2. Three 'must read' papers by Ferenczi   5
  3. Children, animals, and poetry   6
  4. Alternate professions   7
  5. Lifestyle requirements   8
  6. Silent sacrifices   9
  7. Seeking diverse supervision   10
  8. Setting up an office   11

9.	A mysterious rug	12
10.	Entering a world of ambiguity	14
11.	Reading, reading, and reading	15
12.	Borrowed faith	16

Part II: Principles

13.	Mental health vs. mental illness	19
14.	A mentally healthy person	20
15.	Half-sane, half-insane	21
16.	Happy and unhappy children	22
17.	Peek-a-boo	23
18.	Hunger, vision, and the rhythms of nature	24
19.	Learning from children	25
20.	The non-human envelope	26
21.	Toy shops are not for kids	27
22.	Religion vs. spirituality	28
23.	Sex–aggression–sex	29
24.	Metapsychology	30
25.	Two major updates on metapsychology	32
26.	'Bad' death instinct, 'good' death instinct	34

27.	Six misunderstandings about death	36
28.	Three reactions to separation	38
29.	Two griefs that last a lifetime	39
30.	What happens to the deceased's possessions?	40
31.	A crowded preconscious	42
32.	Receiving vs. taking	43
33.	Reaction formation and undoing	44
34.	Even Unabomber …	45
35.	Double bind	46
36.	The unknown, the unmet, and the unlived	47
37.	Where does an aborted childhood go?	48
38.	Being emotional vs. being sentimental	50
39.	Feeling 'at home'	51
40.	Who should change?	52
41.	Toxic nobility	53
42.	Basic trust, earned trust, and mutual trust	54
43.	Good-enough revenge	55
44.	Where the ego was …	56
45.	Two 'great crimes'	57
46.	Detachment theory	59

Part III: Practice

47. The day and time for the first appointment — 63
48. Abstinence — 64
49. The sacred nature of the clinical space — 65
50. Restroom — 66
51. Where is Rome? — 67
52. Hearing is essential for listening — 69
53. Floating couch — 70
54. Does the analyst's gender matter? — 71
55. No 'correct' way of laying on the couch — 72
56. Handling patients' questions — 73
57. Doodling etc. — 74
58. Addressing the analyst by his or her title — 75
59. Not asking about actual sex — 76
60. Before and after — 77
61. About defecation and feces — 78
62. Diminishing frequency of sessions — 79
63. Chronic lateness — 81
64. The use of a deliberately wrong interpretation — 82
65. Small gifts given by immigrant patients — 83

66.	Refusing to listen to certain kinds of material	84
67.	Being special	86
68.	Pleasure and mental illness	87
69.	'Insane chemistry'	88
70.	Demystification	90
71.	Imaginary interlocutors	92
72.	When not to give the bill to a patient?	93
73.	Humility	95
74.	Which form of racism is worse?	96
75.	Masochistic funnel	97
76.	The novelist and the poet	98
77.	Analyst's boredom	99
78.	Analyst's financial status	100
79.	Where does the analyst look?	101
80.	Insight addiction	102
81.	Three different outcomes	103
82.	Why not this at the end?	104
83.	The fate of the analyst's bills	106
84.	Uttering an adult patient's first name	107
85.	Procrastination and nail-biting	108

86. Stillness	109
87. Cats, not dogs	110
88. Countertransference sublimation	112
89. Financial extremes	113
90. The analyst's dog	114

Part IV: Profession

91. The second beard	117
92. Psychiatry and psychoanalysis	118
93. Do we need a prefix to 'psychoanalysis'?	120
94. Jewish psychoanalysis, Christian psychoanalysis	121
95. Pauses	122
96. Writers and non-writers	124
97. Analysts' memoirs	125
98. Was Bion Hindu?	126
99. PEP vetting	128
100. Age-specific writing	129
101. The 'domestication' of analysis	130
102. Childless child analysts	131
103. Three tips for supervisors	132

104.	Non-analyst friends	133
105.	The future of psychoanalysis	134
106.	Blood killing	135
107.	Un-associated and un-affiliated	136
108.	Analysts turned gurus	137
109.	Taboos	138
110.	The analyst's funeral	139
111.	Alternate pathways	140

Acknowledgments   *141*
About the author   *143*
Name index   *145*

Introduction

Brevity has a link with passing time, hence with mortality, and, as Shakespeare famously declared, it is 'the soul of wit.' This unexpected coupling imparts a certain wry and definitive quality to that which is stated briefly. A sweet irony of this very sort suffuses the short pieces contained in the pages of this book. Denuded of jargon, bibliographic citations, and footnotes, these proto-essays seek to highlight one omission, underscore one tension, and challenge one assumption at a time. The hope integral to this approach is that the reader would be persuaded to think, concur, refute, and refine the proposals offered here and by such effort join the author in furthering the cause and message of our much loved field: psychoanalysis.

Part I

Preparation

'The repressed exercises a continuous pressure in the direction of the conscious.'

Sigmund Freud (1856–1939)

1

Reading Freud

In many *au courant* psychoanalytic training programs (and some old ones striving for a sort of rejuvenation) in the United States, reading Freud is marginalized and rendered optional. This is unfortunate since his work is an inexhaustible font of psychoanalytic knowledge. The fact that some of his ideas were phallocentric, Eurocentric, and otherwise ill-founded must not serve as a license to throw the proverbial baby out with the bathwater.

While one ought to read more—much more—, a basic minimum when it comes to Freud's work includes the following seminal papers from each realm of his contributions. (a) *Metapsychological realm*: The interpretation of dreams, The unconscious, Repression, Negation, Splitting of the ego in the process of defense, and Beyond the pleasure principle. (b) *Developmental realm*: Two principles of mental functioning, On narcissism, Dissolution of Oedipus complex, and The universal tendency towards debasement of the love object. (c) *Clinical realm:* A specific type of object choice made by men, Mourning and melancholia, Papers on technique, Some character types met with during clinical work, and Inhibitions, symptoms, and anxiety. (d) *Cultural realm*: Creative writers and day dreaming, The future of an illusion, and Civilization and its discontents.

2

Three 'must read' papers by Ferenczi

Long before the contemporary contributions of Jody Messler Davies and Bessel van der Kolk, the great Hungarian psychoanalyst Sándor Ferenczi had laid down the groundwork for understanding and ameliorating childhood psychic trauma. From his extensive publications on this topic, three truly outstanding papers are (a) *on rejection and neglect*: 'The unwelcome child and his death instinct,' (b) *on sexual abuse*: 'Confusion of tongues between adults and the child,' and (c) *on addressing the injured core* of traumatized adults: 'Child analysis in the analysis of adults.' Together this triumvirate constitutes the best psychoanalysis has to offer vis-à-vis childhood psychic trauma. It must be read and re-read by all those who aspire to enter the field.

3

Children, animals, and poetry

Applicants for psychoanalytic training need to have well-grounded capacities for psychological-mindedness, altruism, curiosity, empathy, patience, benign regression, and non-exploitative relationships. One way of assessing these attributes is to ask the applicants to describe their feelings about children, animals, and poetry. Exploration along these lines reveals the applicants' underlying penchant for the exercise of the abilities listed above and also provides information about the suppleness of their language and their openness to nonverbal discourse.

4

Alternate professions

Significant inferences can be drawn from the answer someone applying for psychoanalytic training gives to the following question: 'What sort of work would you do if for some reason you were totally barred from the mental health field?' It is encouraging to hear the applicant say that they might consider becoming a schoolteacher or vocational counselor since interpersonal contact and helpfulness to others characterize these lines of work as well. However, if the applicant's choice of an alternate profession involves theoretical physics or nanotechnology, one has to wonder—privately and without wincing—about the solidity of their avowed aim to become a psychoanalyst.

5

Lifestyle requirements

Someone wanting to devote their life to practicing intensive psychotherapy or psychoanalysis needs to keep in mind the following lifestyle requirements that come with this choice: (a) renunciation of the pleasure of gossiping and of aspirations to be the 'man about town,' (b) no participation in flashy social media, (c) a predictable yearly schedule of vacations and holiday breaks, (d) mostly unchanging personal appearance, and (e) commitment to stay in the same city for pretty much the rest of one's life.

6
Silent sacrifices

Those who seek to spend their lives practicing psychoanalysis or intensive psychotherapy must know that helping professions often necessitate what David Sachs has termed 'silent sacrifices.' These acts of quiet renunciations (e.g., not attending a dinner in order to take care of a clinical emergency) and unannounced altruism (e.g., reducing fees for a patient in economic downfall) also characterize the practice of psychoanalysis. The dictates of an archaic professional superego (e.g., What would 'they' say?) or emotionally charged intrusions of theory (e.g., Am I being masochistic here?) must not be allowed to preclude such gestures of human decency and care.

7

Seeking diverse supervision

In seeking supervision, the trainee should try to find senior clinicians of varying persuasions, different genders, and those working with diverse clinical populations. Being supervised by a child analyst on an adult case, for instance, helps the trainee acquire a somewhat different voice to interpret than he or she would receive from a supervisor who works exclusively with adult patients.

8

Setting up an office

While setting up a clinical office, the prospective analyst must learn to blend his or her personal esthetics with certain requirements derived from a deep understanding of the psychoanalytic theory and technique. Not possessing such knowledge at this juncture, the individual would be helped by perusing the papers on the components and layout of the analyst's office by Henrik Carpelan, Jon Mills, and Salman Akhtar, as well as the recent book on this very topic by Mark Gerald. In any case, the analyst's office should have home-like comfort, predictability, and simplicity. It should neither be spartan (e.g., with completely bare walls) nor ostentatious (e.g., with a large grand piano or a running water fountain in it). Both extremes render the space more noticeable than it should be. This spoils silent 'holding' which, in turn, makes 'relating' difficult, to use Donald Winnicott's phraseology.

9

A mysterious rug

In describing a space suitable for doing psychoanalytic work, Donald Winnicott said 'The work was to be done in a room, not a passage, that was quiet and not liable to sudden unpredictable sounds, yet not dead quiet and not free from ordinary house noises. This room would be lit properly, but not by a light staring in the face, and not by a variable light. The room would certainly not be dark and it would be comfortably warm … and probably a rug and some water would be available.' Everything in this description makes sense except the mention of a 'rug.' It is unlikely that the 'rug' Winnicott had in mind was akin to the Turkish carpets languishing on Freud's couch. More likely is that he meant a soft blanket which the patient could use as a transitional object or a defensive cloak if needed. Such interpretation of 'rug' seems closer to the warmth of Winnicott's style, to his emphasis on holding, and is better aligned with the phrase 'would be available.' But then why not just say 'a soft blanket'? Why 'a rug'?

10

Entering a world of ambiguity

Those who aspire to take intensive psychotherapy or psychoanalysis as their life-long vocation must prepare themselves to enter the world of ambiguity. Uncertainty reigns in this world and numerous dialectical tensions exist. An admittedly incomplete list of such tensions includes those between determinism and free will, between conscious and unconscious, between nature and nurture, between rational and irrational, between expression and concealment, between separation and merger, between collaboration and defiance, and behind all this, between life and death.

11
Reading, reading, and reading

Human nature is hard, if not impossible, to understand. Too many variables, veils, and variations hide, alter, shape, color, embellish, and minimize what there is to know. Anyone taking human mind as their realm of understanding and praxis must therefore devote himself or herself to a lifetime of reading. Such reading would mostly involve the texts of psychology, psychiatry, and psychoanalysis but would often need to make forays into the works of anthropology, sociology, theology, fiction, and poetry. Those who shrug off this heavy responsibility by saying that they are intending only to be clinicians and not academicians overlook the fact that treating patients is not merely a craft. The harvest of therapeutic enterprise is nourished and enhanced by experience but even more so by knowledge acquired from reading.

12

Borrowed faith

Prospective trainees in the field of psychoanalysis and intensive psychotherapy need to know and accept the unpleasant fact that, for a very long period of time, they will lack confidence about their clinical interventions. Trust in their own ability will develop only gradually, and for many years they will have to survive on 'borrowed faith.' The 'lenders' of such assuredness include: (a) clinical material published by experienced psychoanalysts, (b) the advice of one's supervisors, (c) the internalization of one's analysts 'confident optimism,' to use an expression of Therese Benedek, and (d) the corrective input of one's patients. Drawing strength and knowledge from these sources shall make the journey from 'expectable hesitation' to 'earned faith' easier.

Part II

Principles

'It is important for the analysis that the analyst should be able to meet the patient as far as possible with almost inexhaustible patience, understanding, goodwill, and kindness.'

Sándor Ferenczi (1873–1933)

13

Mental health vs. mental illness

The difference between a mentally healthy and a mentally troubled person rests upon two simple variables: (a) the mentally healthy person has a bigger healthy and a smaller ill part; the opposite is true of the mentally ill individual, and (b) in the mentally healthy individual, the sane part acts like a loving and protective older sibling towards the ill part whereas in the mentally ill individual the sick part dominates, terrorizes, and gaslights the healthy part.

14

A mentally healthy person

An individual is considered largely mentally healthy if he or she can (a) distinguish between what is real and what is unreal, (b) accept that some things are impossible, (c) live with the fact that a few other things, while possible, are prohibited, (d) maintain closeness with others without surrendering his or her self entirely and be separate from them without becoming painfully alone, (e) bring affection and lust together in the form of romantic love, (f) retain a consistent and coherent character, (g) experience empathy, humility, and gratitude, and (h) display the capacities for work and play.

15

Half-sane, half-insane

Manfred Bleuler, the son of the immortal Eugen Bleuler and himself a distinguished psychiatrist, once warned against the enthusiasm to eradicate schizophrenia from the world. He said that the 'schizophrenia gene' serves a useful purpose. People who are 'sane' lack the desire to make great contributions to humanity and people who are 'insane' lack the capacity to do so. The world is enriched, improved, and run by those who are 'half-sane–half-insane,' and these people most likely possess some muted variant of the 'schizophrenia gene.' Eradicating schizophrenia altogether is therefore likely to make the world stagnate, lose inventiveness, and undergo decay.

16

Happy and unhappy children

Most happy children grow up to be adults with traits of compassion, moral clarity, generosity, gratitude, and love for family and friends. They are society's source of 'good' people. Most unhappy children lack such capacities upon growing up but can turn out to be quite interesting, creative, and highly accomplished people. They are society's source of 'great people.'

17

Peek-a-boo

Peek-a-boo is ubiquitous. The game whereby a mother hides her face momentarily from her young child and then reveals it to the chortling joy of the latter is played all over the world. This universal prevalence is most likely due to the game's ability to convey multilayered psychological messages to both the baby and the mother. (a) *To the baby*, it transmits the concept of 'object permanence' (i.e., things continue to exist even when not in sight). It also teaches the baby that he or she can 'survive,' even if for a very short time, in the absence of the mother. (b) *To the mother*, the game teaches the art of letting go of the child, of permitting the child to grow apart, and thus prepares her for the day when he or she would ultimately leave her.

18

Hunger, vision, and the rhythms of nature

Three factors are responsible for the self-absorbed omnipotent infant's move towards the reality principle and learning that there is more to this world than its own self. These include (1) the baby's realization that while tension release from the needs of urination and defecation are under self-control, pangs of hunger and the consequent longing for the breast are beyond his or her omnipotence, (2) the gap between the baby's visual reach (usually eighteen to twenty inches) and his or her tactile (usually six to eight inches) reach ruptures its megalomaniac self-sufficiency, and (3) circadian rhythms of sleep–wakefulness and the nature-initiated shifts between days and nights impart a sense of 'proto-humility' to the baby. Working in unison, these three variables pull the infant out of its pleasure-principle–spun cocoon into the open skies of the reality principle and object relations.

19

Learning from children

Fort-Da, the game his eighteen-month-old grandson was playing by pushing a wooden reel out of sight and then pulling it back, taught Freud about the efforts human beings make to master separation anxiety. While this particular instance got enshrined in psychoanalytic history, the field has paid inadequate attention to how children affect their caregivers, often making remarkable contributions to the adults' mental health. Anecdotal reports abound with people giving up smoking, drinking alcohol, and physical abuse upon the insistence and intervention of their offspring. Less dramatic but no less salutary are the cultural corrections children of immigrants make for their parents' befuddled egos.

20

The non-human envelope

While the dynamically fluid content of the human mind involves relationships (real or imaginary) with other human beings, its structural integrity depends upon non-human elements that include time, space, animals, things, money, and God. Together these six components form an 'envelope' that contains the experiential scribblings of mental life. Rupture of this envelope (e.g., upon immigration, during the Covid pandemic) fills the psyche with mental pain and disorienting anxiety.

21

Toy shops are not for kids

However generous and indulgent their parents might be, children are unhappy, if not in tears, upon leaving a toy shop. This is because they feel overstimulated by the profusion of things to play with, have had to choose just one (or two) from the plethora available and leave so many tempting things behind. It is therefore not a good idea to take children to toy shops. It is much better for the parents to go, select a toy with empathy for the child, and bring it home as a joyous surprise.

22

Religion vs. spirituality

The differences between religion and spirituality include: (1) religion insists upon God's existence, spirituality does not, (2) religion proposes life after death in one form or the other, spirituality makes no such promise, (3) religion divides people into groups, spirituality unites the entire humanity, (4) religion prescribes rituals and prohibits certain actions, spirituality does not, (5) religion puts animals and inanimate objects beneath human beings, spirituality sees dignity in everything and denounces such stratification, (6) religion relies upon texts and scriptures, spirituality on compassion and earned wisdom.

23

Sex–aggression–sex

By and large, it is true that sexual hunger, seductiveness with a sense of urgency, promiscuity, and lasciviousness are painted veils against inner desperation, rage, hate, and cruelty. It is also true that authority conflicts, irritability, and argumentativeness are frequent defenses against prohibited erotic desires. Another way of saying this is that sex on the surface masks aggression and aggression on the surface hides sex. The former configuration is typical of perverts, the latter of neurotics.

24

Metapsychology

Freud called his triple-faceted approach to mental phenomena *metapsychology*. The three 'perspectives' he delineated were topographic, dynamic, and economic. (a) *Topographic perspective* questioned what was known and what was unknown to the subject, what was conscious and what was unconscious in his or her experience; this point of view 'deepened' the material under consideration. (b) *Dynamic perspective* sought to trace the various forces that contributed to a fantasy, dream, daydream, or behavior; these forces could emanate from desire, moral imperatives, or reality. (c) *Economic perspective* tracked the direction, amount, and intensity of psychic energy expended in any real or imaginary action; its concern was the quantitative dimension of mental phenomena. Many 'perspectives' were added later but only two survived the test of time: genetic and adaptive. (d) *Genetic perspective* links past with present and especially childhood with adulthood; it unearths origins of things. (e) *Adaptive perspective* underscores the 'benefit' or 'usefulness' of all imagination and behavior, including that which causes trouble for self and others. In modified and refined forms, these five perspectives constitute contemporary metapsychology. There is no psychoanalysis without it.

25

Two major updates on metapsychology

Of the five perspectives of metapsychology (topographic, dynamic, economic, genetic, and adaptive), two need serious updates. One is the economic and the other the genetic perspective. (a) *Economic perspective*, based upon antiquated notions of psychic energy, has been largely discarded in psychoanalysis. The fact, however, is that quantitative concepts still suffuse its clinical work. Analysts constantly speak of 'overstimulation,' 'deficit,' 'hyper-vigilance,' 'excessive narcissism,' 'optimal distance,' and so on. The old economic perspective needs to be modified to accommodate such ideas. This would essentially mean introducing 'too muchness' and 'too littleness' as basic parameters that determine what 'amount' of a feeling or behavior is detrimental to self-coherence and the retention of healthy object relations. (b) *Genetic perspective* should be re-named 'genetic-developmental' perspective in order to underscore that not only the past (especially childhood) shapes the present but the present, with its fresh ego achievements, assimilates the past in a modified way that contains an influential layer of new fantasies and new capacities.

26

'Bad' death instinct, 'good' death instinct

It is well known that Freud introduced the concept of 'death instinct' in his 1920 paper 'Beyond the pleasure principle.' What has gone unrecognized is that Freud used the expression in a plural form ('death instincts') many times in this paper and in his other writings. This, most likely, refers to 'bad' (destructive) and 'good' (stress-receiving) forms of this instinct. Each form has its own outcomes.

The outcomes of the 'bad' death instinct include: (a) projection, leading to the creation of 'bad objects' against whom justifiable aggression can be directed; (b) binding by the life instinct giving rise to the 'hard-wired' capacity in human beings to draw pleasure from pain; (c) dripping inside the body and contributing to the development of autoimmune diseases; (d) getting directed at mental functions, causing attacks on linking, and fueling what André Green has called 'the work of the negative.' *The outcomes of 'good' death instinct* include: (a) the capacity to lie fallow, (b) states where self is lost via an 'oceanic' merger with the universe or dissolves in the erotic ecstasy of sexual orgasm, (c) genuinely blank silence, and (d) dreamless sleep.

27

Six misunderstandings about death

Psychoanalysis contains many contradictory, confusing, and incorrect ideas about death. Here are some of them: (a) It asserts that the unconscious does not believe in its death while simultaneously proposing that the unconscious contains 'instinctual representatives' (including, presumably, those of the death instinct): (b) it makes little differentiation between an untimely death and death at the end of a long and deeply satisfying life; (c) it puts premium on psychic reality but displays a peculiar literalness in holding that death always follows life. This is not true. Many people die (psychologically) first and then live. Their lives are characterized by extraordinary stoicism, self-destructive hedonism, and, at times, search for what Milan Kundera has called 'Great Immortality'; (d) it suggests that fear of death is ubiquitous, an idea that flies in the face of death being viewed by many as a longed-for eternal rest; the Eurocentric bias in such conceptualization is not acknowledged; (e) it assumes that only the orphaned, the elderly, and the physically ill talk of death in clinical sessions. This belief is derived from a cultural blind spot which prevents discerning the ubiquitous nature of death-related themes in patients' associations; (f) it takes the appearance of death in patients' associations towards the end of their analyses as a metaphor. This may be correct but it leaves no space for considering that such talk may also be the patients' last ditch effort to discuss their and the analysts' mortality.

28

Three reactions to separation

For those who have forgotten and for those who never encountered it, Freud's astute delineation of three emotional responses to separation is worth recounting: (a) *sadness* when the person who left was not needed for one's psychic integrity but was deeply loved and desired, (b) *anxiety* when that person served as a major support and helped maintain one's sanity and coherence, and (c) *mental pain—Seelenschmerz* in Freud's phraseology—when the departed person was experienced as a part of one's self; such separation is akin to an amputation.

29

Two griefs that last a lifetime

The loss of a parent (especially the mother) during early childhood and the loss of an adolescent (or young adult) offspring constitute two griefs that are never 'resolved.' The pain and yearning become tempered with passage of time but the wound never turns into a scar. Even the best analytic treatment, while providing significant relief from derivative (and often unrecognized) symptomatology, does not result in such transformation.

30

What happens to the deceased's possessions?

Most human beings accumulate a lot of objects over their lifetime. These range from big and expensive items like houses, cars, jewelry, and furniture to the mundane utensils of daily living such as clothes, pots and pans, shoes, fork and knives, towels, bed sheets, toothbrush, eye glasses, towels, and so on. Upon an individual's death, such physical possessions are divided into three categories: (a) things that are thrown, (b) things that are given away to charity organizations or poor and distant relatives, and (c) things that are kept within the nuclear family and passed on as heirlooms.

In circumstances where the bereaved cannot accomplish a healthy resolution of mourning, (a) the disposal of the deceased's possessions is either immediate or long delayed, (b) the three categories get blurred, and (c) the things that are kept get imbued with stinging ambivalence. Turning into what Vamık Volkan has termed 'linking objects,' such things can't be displayed and used (this stirs up the pain of loss) but cannot be discarded either (this becomes tantamount to murder). One is stuck with them forever, unless a wise therapist helps the perennial mourner to bring these objects to the treatment sessions and thaw their frozen status.

31

A crowded preconscious

Some things, even if conflictual, do not succumb to repression and continue to exist as clumsy furniture in the psychic corridor called 'preconscious.' Having had an abortion is one such thing. Belonging to any type of minority, being an immigrant, losing a parent in childhood, and having been raped in adulthood are among others. Such 'presences' can clog the preconscious and become a source of cumulative trauma.

32

Receiving vs. taking

Some individuals have difficulty in receiving gifts, favors, care, and compliments. Receiving is difficult for them since it stirs up deep-seated wishes for taking which are suffused with pain and anxiety. As children, when they wanted to take, there was no one to give, or the giver mercilessly deprived them. This resulted in the intensification of their hunger while also eroding their confidence in asking for things. Taking became anathema and any experience that mobilized wishes to take was strenuously avoided.

33

Reaction formation and undoing

Reaction formation reverses the 'aim' (to hate, to kill, to desire, to love) of an instinct while retaining its 'object' (mother, father, spouse, child). It is a rigid and once-and-for-all sort of operation and changes the character of the individual; a man intending to cause harm, for instance, becomes a relentless philanthropist. *Undoing*, in contrast, refers to a psychic or motor act performed to cancel the effects of another act that has occurred in fantasy. It tackles one impulse at a time and 'cancels' it by an action opposite to it. The relationship between reaction formation and undoing is akin to that between a season and weather!

34

Even Unabomber …

The current psychiatric categorization of loners into two types is based on the ground that one ('avoidant') shuns human contact due to fear of rejection while the other ('schizoid') lacks the desire for such contact. This proposal has two problems: (a) it does not take into account that people can stay aloof due to fear of being accepted and loved as well, and (b) by carving out a class of loners who actually do not want interaction and affection, it negates the fact that all human beings—hermits and hobos included—desire interpersonal contact. Even Ted Kaczynski, the notoriously reclusive Unabomber, was writing letters to people and wanted his thoughts published in newspapers with a nationwide circulation. He clearly was reaching out to people and wanted to be 'rescued' from his isolated hideout.

35

Double bind

Described by Gregory Bateson, 'double bind' is a form of communication that leaves its recipient trapped between two bad choices and with no way out of the conundrum. Two outstanding examples of such imprisoning messages are a roadside placard saying 'Ignore this sign' and an inebriated father telling his son to never listen to him when he is drunk. A subtler manifestation of 'double bind' is when someone says 'I want you to bring such and such thing for me when you visit though I know that you will most likely forget it.' This puts the listener in a quandary: if I don't take the thing then I deprive him but if I do I disprove his prediction. I turn out to be bad either way. This entrapment is the essence of a 'double bind' according to Bateson who declared it to be truly crazy-making.

36

The unknown, the unmet, and the unlived

Encounters with strangers are hardly restricted to external reality. They exist in the internal world as well. The experience of meeting someone (or something) strange on an intrapsychic level comes in three forms: (a) *the unknown* (which includes the repressed material and other contents of the unconscious), (b) *the unmet* (which includes the derivatives of 'family romance' and the imaginary present and future of unborn and/or long dead siblings and children), and (c) *the unlived* (which contains consciously known but un-actualized self-representations). All this has significant existential and clinical implications.

37

Where does an aborted childhood go?

In the United States, infants hardly sleep in bed with their mothers, weeks-old babies are sent to 'day-care,' toddlers are whisked away to 'pre-nurseries' and 'pre-schools,' school-age children are transformed into 'latchkey kids' and expected to carry their own bags while at airports and train stations, and adolescents are mandated to leave the parental home. Such hastening of psychic development causes a massive repression of innocence, wonder, awe, kinship with animals, and the good old 'oral dependency' that used to characterize childhood. However, in accordance with Freud's dictum that 'the repressed exerts a continuous upward pressure in the direction of consciousness,' the banished American childhood finds derivative expressions in the nation's culture. Talking animals (translate, children's imaginary companions) take over television commercials, masses walk on streets drinking from water (translate, milk) bottles with eyes glued to cellphone screens (translate, maternal breast), and seemingly mature adults are irresistibly drawn to animated movies and Hollywood blockbusters that extol superheroes. That an aborted childhood is being resuscitated via all this technical wizardry and unending psychic hydration, however, goes unnoticed.

38

Being emotional vs. being sentimental

In talking of emotional life, psychoanalysis uses two expressions: 'affective' and 'affectualized.' Ordinary English calls them 'emotional' and 'sentimental,' respectively. The former indicates that appropriate and, at times, intense feelings are associated with a thought or memory or experience. The latter refers to a maudlin attitude about the existence of those very affects. To put it bluntly, being sentimental means being emotional about being emotional.

39

Feeling 'at home'

Feeling 'at home' involves a combination of psychosomatic relaxation, freedom from formalities, and a non-noisy sense of entitlement. The capacity to experience this feeling state emanates from unquestioned belonging to one's childhood home and from unpretentious, ongoing care by one's parents. Those who were fortunate in this regard feel 'at home' in their own homes and can more or less re-create the feeling at other places as well. Those who were not so lucky but were helped by distant relatives or neighbors, feel 'at home' only in their friends' houses and in hotels. And, there are those who were orphaned or otherwise abandoned by parents; they do not feel 'at home' anywhere, including within their own bodies and minds. Forever, they yearn for a home that never existed. They wander, travel widely, try to settle down but somehow feel compelled to move again. They are the 'seekers'!

40

Who should change?

The fact that one does not have the power to change others, and those others are not motivated to change themselves anyway, forces one to the realization that, in order to 'improve' one's life, one has to change oneself. This depressing awareness is paradoxically a sign of hope and possibility of betterment.

41

Toxic nobility

It is noble to make a concerted effort at being good, but trying to become noble is not good. One ends up sequestering a whole lot of aggression, falls psychosomatically ill, becomes masochistic and quasi-addicted to passive death wishes towards self and others.

42

Basic trust, earned trust, and mutual trust

There exists a trust–mistrust tension between an early immigrant and his host community. The severity of it depends upon the magnitude of differences in the two parties that range from skin color and religion to historical and political variables. Under fortunate circumstances and with passage of time, this tension diminishes. The pre-migration stability of confident expectation in the immigrant's character and salutary exchange between him or her and the host community help their relationship advance to what can be called 'earned trust.' This, in turn, gradually yields sustained harmony and 'mutual trust.'

43

Good-enough revenge

Even though ordinary decency, with or without the hues of religious benevolence, suggests that taking revenge is not good, psychoanalysis contains the notion of a 'good-enough' revenge. Such revenge (a) should be taken only once, (b) should be considerably less 'bloody' than what is desired in fantasy, (c) should not be self-injurious, and (d) should ideally lead to some social benefit.

44

Where the ego was …

The celebrated statement by Freud, that as a consequence of analytic treatment, 'where id was, there ego shall be,' highlights the laboriously earned rational control over unruly passions. The statement is elegant, powerful, and correct. Yet it feels incomplete. After much thinking, I have come to believe that a complete version of it might read something like 'where id was, their ego shall be and ego shall also be where superego was.' After all, the renunciation of incestuous and murderous omnipotence in an analyzed person is not because of his or her enhanced compliance with the Torah or the Bible or the Quran but because of their enriched appreciation of the value of familial bonds and friendships, all of which will be destroyed by their lack of restraint.

45

Two 'great crimes'

The 1916 declaration by Freud that incest and parricide are the two 'great human crimes' gives testimony simultaneously to his genius and its phallocentric limitations. Incest is certainly terrible since it destroys familial links without which human existence is unbearable. But parricide? Why only the murder of the father? Is killing the mother or, for that matter, a sibling or a child, fine?

It is my conviction that Freud's phallocentric bias cast a thick shadow upon most developmental and psychopathological notions he came up; often the result was narrow, inaccurate, and, at times, a bit silly. The inclusion of parricide instead of the more inclusive 'murder' is one such instance. Had Freud stated that the two great human crimes are incest and murder, it would have unshackled the proposal from its male oedipal confines and rendered it universally applicable and far more true.

Incest is a 'great human crime' because it defiles family and murder because it destroys reality (of someone's existence). Both are destructive of our filiation with human civilization.

46

Detachment theory

With the jettisoning of religious belief, dissolution of joint and extended families, skyrocketing divorce rates, shamelessly rushed childhood, and relegation of the care of infants and toddlers to people other than the mother, loneliness and desperate object hunger (often masked by pseudo self-sufficiency) came to clinical attention in the West; systematic investigation needed and, in a dialectical loop, produced, a set of hypotheses. These got collectively called the *attachment theory*. In the East, the situation was opposite. Family members were enmeshed, a unitary self was not solidly established, collectivism abounded, God was everywhere, and aloneness was a mirage. Reaction to this was to declare the self ephemeral and the material world an illusion. Lacking psychoanalysis and yet needing to grapple with the longed-for solitude, philosophical traditions extolled the virtues of stoicism, lack of desire, and non-attachment. This could be called a *detachment theory*.

Such notions also appeared, albeit quietly, in psychoanalytic theory of development, psychopathology, and treatment. Thus the phenomena of weaning, toilet training, oedipal renunciation, adolescent disengagement from archaic parental imagos, midlife 'downsizing' and retirement can all be viewed as normative steps of detachment. Desperate clinging to supportive others and erotomanic stalking reflect deficit of detachment and narcissistic lack of empathy and sociopathic callousness its excess. In the treatment situation too, the intensity of transference, the tenacity of beliefs, and addiction to repetition betrayed what was once called 'adhesive libido' and the pallor of transference, the 'as-if' character pathology, and easy replacement of objects (including the analyst) pointed to an excess of detachment. In the end, it seems psychoanalysis does not have to 'invent' a heuristic twin of 'attachment theory.' It already has a set of observations and hypotheses that need to be grouped under the designation of a 'detachment theory.'

Part III

Practice

'Side by side with the destructive impulses in the unconscious mind both of the child and of the adult, there exists a profound urge to make sacrifices, in order to help and put right loved people who in phantasy have been harmed or destroyed.'

Melanie Klein (1882–1960)

47

The day and time for the first appointment

In setting up the very first appointment—generally on the phone—it seems advisable to let the prospective patient choose the day and time for it. Rather than 'I can see you next Tuesday at 2 pm,' it is preferable to ask 'How soon would you like this appointment to be?' or 'Is there a particular day and time of the week that is better for you to come in?' This way of responding lets the patient exert some control over the situation, a measure that restores respect and dignity to the patient just when his or her need for help is eroding his self-esteem.

48

Abstinence

When Freud declared that the work of psychoanalysis 'must be carried out in abstinence,' he meant that the analyst should not gratify transference-based desires of the patient. Astutely, he expanded the notion beyond physical deprivation to include the avoidance of emotional actualization of such wishes. But what about the analyst's smoking cigars during analytic sessions? Or cigarettes? Or drinking coffee? Or casting surreptitious glances at an attractive patient on the couch? Making unnecessary self-disclosures? Asking the patient for business tips? Telling jokes because they are just so goddamned funny? While psychoanalytic glossaries do not place restriction on such activities under the rubric of 'abstinence,' it is clear that they should.

49

The sacred nature of the clinical space

Psychoanalysts must not drink alcohol, smoke pot, use drugs, masturbate, or have sex in their offices. Memories linger, actions cast shadows, and sights and sounds crystallize into apparitions. Sacredness of the therapeutic space is lost and the lack of its acknowledgment introduces the undesirable element of untruth in clinical work.

50

Restroom

Most psychoanalysts provide some form of restroom access to the patient regardless of whether their office is at their home or in a professional building. What they forget is that such access should be made explicit at the very outset of their contact. This makes the patient's occasional use of the facility an integral part of the therapeutic frame, without creating a contraindication for analyzing the neurotic fantasies and uses, if any, of such provision. The situation is akin to showing an overnight house guest the door to the bathroom he or she can use.

51

Where is Rome?

The old saying 'When in Rome, do as the Romans do' has been unblinkingly translated to mean that the patients ought to accommodate to their analysts' cultural and aesthetic proclivities. In other words, the analyst is the Roman and his office Rome.

But is it? Really? The fact is that both analysts and patients not only bring their pathos but also their ethos to the clinical situation. Thus, differences between patients and analysts might crop up along the ethos-related variables of time, reverence for authority, optimal distance, politics, money, use of first names, collectivism vs. individualism, and so on. Such differences need to be dealt by the analyst with empathy and respect as well judicious alterations of the therapeutic frame (with or without exploratory-interpretive follow-up). In essence, both parties in the clinical dyad should be viewed as potential Romans and the psychic space that facilitates therapeutic alliance as Rome.

52

Hearing is essential for listening

It is distressing to come across psychoanalysts who have mild to moderate hearing loss and do not use hearing aids. More upsetting is that the impairment is treated with polite indifference by their colleagues who take no action to combat the situation. Both parties ignore the potential strain this can put on that analyst's patients.

53

Floating couch

When the analytic couch is placed in an office so that none of its four sides are in contact with a wall, it is referred to as a 'floating couch.' An eye-popping example of this is the couch that is smack in the center of the office, with the nearest walls on all four sides of it being many, many feet away. For reasons not fully understood but perhaps involving defiance of conventionality in the analyst and deeper regression in the 'unsupported' patient, this arrangement is often associated with gross boundary violations.

54

Does the analyst's gender matter?

Does it make a substantive difference to the process and outcome of treatment if the psychoanalyst is a man or a woman? The truth is that the field cannot satisfactorily answer this question, though there are many speculations, opinions, anecdotes, and hypotheses. Further conundrum results from the fact that many male analysts (e.g., Ferenczi) are more maternal and many female analysts (e.g., Klein) more paternal.

55

No 'correct' way of laying on the couch

Patients are expected to lay down on the couch facing away from the analyst and most of them do so. Once in a rare while a patient puts his or her feet at the 'head end' and head at the 'foot end' of the couch and lies looking squarely at the analyst. Instead of the 'sharp reprimand' given by Freud to patients who did not close the door behind them as they entered his clinical chamber, this behavior needs to be met with tolerance, curiosity, and analytic exploration. The same applies to instances where patients stay totally motionless on the couch with their hands neatly folded and resting on their belly, regularly keep one foot on the floor, adopt a sideways sleeping posture, or fold their knees up and never fully occupy the couch. The analyst must remember that there is no 'correct' way of lying on the couch and each posture has its own meanings, its own purposes, and its own concealing and communicative functions.

56

Handling patients' questions

When it comes to patients' questions, the psychoanalyst needs to (a) maintain an attitude that does not discourage patients from asking questions, (b) know the difference between responding and answering, (c) answer schedule-related and 'conversation-grease' questions readily, (d) following Herbert Schlesinger's counsel, regard most other questions as patients' answers to deeper curiosities which warrant exploration, and (e) refuse to answer certain questions (e.g., 'Were you abused as a child?') but explain his stance on the basis that answering them could risk altering or even reversing the therapeutic gradient in the dyad; following this, he needs to resume the usual analytic posture of investigation and interpretation.

57

Doodling etc.

Freud often picked up an antique statue from his desk and looked at intently as he was listening to a patient on the couch. Anna Freud knitted scarves and shawls during analytic sessions. Other analysts crochet, draw, and doodle while their recumbent patients are revealing their memories, dreams, and fantasies. Such activities enlist the analysts' left brain functions and leave their right brain capacities free for evenly hovering attention. Tightly focusing on a repetitious activity paradoxically enhances the analyst's receptivity to the unconscious communications of the patient.

58

Addressing the analyst by his or her title

Some patients repeatedly use the analyst's professional title even when presumably free-associating. For instance, 'You know, Dr Akhtar, last night I had a dream which …' or 'I really hate my brother, Dr Akhtar, because he is …,' and so on.

While many reasons can account for such a way of talking, strenuous and ongoing defense against developing a transference seems paramount among them. The constant need to remind oneself that one is talking to a professional betrays an underlying dread of wanting an actual (or actualized) relationship and an ego structure too weak to bear its mentalization.

59

Not asking about actual sex

When someone in psychotherapy or psychoanalysis mentions having made love the previous night with their partner, most clinicians assume that they know what the patient is talking about. But do they? Really?

To the best of my knowledge, few therapists respond by saying 'what did you actually do?' Or, 'when you say you made love, what sorts of acts are you including in it?' Or, 'can you describe what an episode of making love typically involves for you?' By being bashful regarding such inquiry, clinicians lose important data about their patients' drive fixations, body fantasies, and longed-for relational scenarios with their partners as whole or part objects.

60

Before and after

Both the written word and handed down oral tradition in clinical psychoanalysis tell us to deal with the patients' material in a certain order. Of course, such 'rules' need to be tailored to each specific clinical situation and titrated in accordance with the patients' ego strength, degree of regression, and solidity of therapeutic alliance. Yet they do carry a certain wisdom and ought not to be ignored or dismissed. Here are five such interventional hierarchies: (1) defense before drive, (2) need before wish, (3) holding before relating, (4) reality before projection, (5) present before past. And, dare I add a most important sixth one? (6) Compassion before technique.

61

About defecation and feces

In the United States, patients undergo psychoanalysis for years and never once mention rituals around their defecation and feelings about their feces. Analysts are complicit by almost never pointing out such omission. This collusion has two roots. (a) One pertains to the massive *cultural repression* of all anal matters and dirtiness in general; the manufacture and sale of cleaning products, deodorants, and perfumes amounts to billions of dollars. Psychoanalysts and their patients are not immune to this mass elimination (pun unintended) of anything smelly and unclean from thought, feeling, and fantasy. (b) The second root involves the *eclipse of the drive theory* and its attendant model of pregenital sexuality. No longer taking the epigenetically unfolding instinctual development seriously, analysts are prone to ditch 'one-person psychology' altogether and become unable to discern drive derivatives in their patients' material.

62

Diminishing frequency of sessions

At the beginning of psychoanalysis, Freud saw his patients six times a week, with each session lasting for fifty minutes. This amounted to 300 minutes of clinical contact between the two parties. Soon Freud lowered the frequency to five sessions per week while maintaining their fifty-minute duration. This brought the total amount of weekly clinical time to 250 minutes.

Later on, analysts, especially those in the United States, began seeing their patients four times a week, for forty-five minute sessions. Mobilized by economic pressures (to put it charitably) or monetary greed (to put it harshly), this practice reduced the total time the patient spent in analysis each week to 180 minutes. And now many analysts consider three times per week as sufficient, which translates into 135 minutes of clinical immersion per week.

What does this downward spiral from 300 through 250 and 180 to 135 minutes per week really indicate? The practice of charging such high fees that make it impossible for analysands to have more frequent sessions? A realistic accommodation to the busy and rushed lives most Americans lead? The analysts' unconscious hatred of psychoanalysis and its slow murder?

63

Chronic lateness

Psychoanalysts either do not know or keep forgetting what Enid Balint said about chronic lateness. It is not a manifestation of negative transference. It emanates from separation anxiety. Difficulty in leaving the place of origin and underestimating the time needed for getting to the destination are the true causes of habitual lateness.

64

The use of a deliberately wrong interpretation

Once, or at best twice, in the opening phase of an analysis, the analyst might deliberately make a wrong, if not absurd, interpretation, followed, in the same breath, by letting the patient know that it was wrong and was intended to demonstrate how it is possible to misuse analytic methodology. Done gently, with mild humor, and with a good-enough therapeutic alliance in place, such intervention paradoxically enhances the credibility of other interventions by the analyst.

65

Small gifts given by immigrant patients

Immigrant patients often bring souvenirs for their therapists upon returning from a visit to their countries of origin. Such gifts should be gracefully accepted and kept in a visible place in the office. These items create a 'little Italy,' a 'little India,' a 'little Greece,' and so on, in the therapist's office which, in turn, helps modestly repair the ecological rupture that haunts the immigrant constantly. In the absence of such artifacts, the clinical space does not feel 'homely' enough.

66

Refusing to listen to certain kinds of material

As early as 1915, Sándor Ferenczi noted that garrulousness and copious speech during clinical sessions can serve as a resistance to analysis. Ella Freeman Sharpe then underscored that speech can become 'instinctualized' (i.e., suffused with affect, hence providing secret gratification of id impulses) and Otto Kernberg emphasized the clinical futility of an enraged patient hurling curse words at the analyst without any capacity left for self-reflection. These observations raise the question whether listening to patients is always 'good' and it might, in some instances, be better to actively and explicitly refuse to listen to the patient. Such intervention seems appropriate (1) when the patient is attempting to pull the analyst into a misalliance, from the very beginning of their contact, (2) when the patient is repeating something *ad nauseam*, (3) when the patient is using speech predominantly for instinctual discharge or narcissistic stabilization, and (4) when the patient is bringing forth a much-analyzed transference in an unconsciously playful manner towards the end of the analysis. I have emphasized that, in general, refusing to listen is a technical strategy that (1) should be utilized only by those with considerable experience in conducting analyses along the customary lines, (2) should be used sparingly and only when one or the other of the indications delineated above is clearly present, (3) should be used after much listening, affirmative interventions, and interpretive work has been done, (4) is reserved for later phases of long analysis, (5) should be made after consultation with a colleague and, if that is not possible, its use must be discussed post hoc with a colleague, (6) should be used after earnest effort has been made to disentangle countertransference temptations from genuine therapeutic intent, (7) requires that its impact upon the patient be looked for and analytically handled.

67

Being special

The sense of being special is generally viewed with skepticism in psychoanalysis. It is considered to be a narcissistic defense against feelings of inferiority or a passive belief arising from undue idealization by the mother during childhood. This might be correct but it leaves no space for the fact that some individuals are really special. Their uniqueness emanates from their remarkable intelligence, exceptional talents, physical beauty and prowess, grit, and, at times, simply from their magnificent ancestry. Validation of this type of specialness (and its attendant burdens) must be a component of technique in working with such individuals.

68

Pleasure and mental illness

Here is a golden rule: the more pleasurable a mental illness is, the less amenable it is to treatment. States of addictions, sexual perversions, hypomania, and pathological narcissism testify to the correctness of such an assertion. The clinician faced with pleasurable psychopathology is, however, left with limited choices: (a) attempt to 'spoil' the pleasure by rendering it egodystonic through confrontative interventions, (b) enlist family support for shaking the patient out of his or her pathological ecstasy, (c) insist upon concomitant group therapy for the same purpose, and (d) wait for aging, a 'spiritual' awakening, or even a personal catastrophe to instill the awareness in the patient that his or her actions are self-destructive and need modification.

69

'Insane chemistry'

Some people are unable to leave a self-centered and demeaning lover because they feel that an incredible and 'insane' chemistry exists between them. Their sexual encounters are 'out-of-this-world,' utterly blissful, and addictive; anything can be overlooked or 'forgiven' to avoid their discontinuation.

What constitutes this 'insane chemistry' becomes only gradually clear and that too upon highly attuned listening and piecemeal deconstruction of the experience. Four components of such intoxicating bondage then become evident: (a) a truly exceptional fit in the concavities and convexities of the lovers' bodies, (b) a deep and gratifying emergence of specific body memories involving skin color, smell, muscle tone, bone contact, and so on, (c) visual and/or verbal messages that reassure against depressive anxieties over one's being unlovable, and (d) a sense of finally resolving—however briefly—a core object relational conflict that has haunted one for years and decades. That all this happens in the setting of an otherwise unsatisfactory relationship can turn the 'insane chemistry' into a source of throbbing ambivalence.

70

Demystification

The invisibility of the analyst sitting behind the couch, coupled with the patient's lack of knowledge about the analyst's personal life, can lead to the treatment process seeming highly mysterious. The taciturn stance of the analyst can also lend the clinical encounter an aura of magic, especially if the analyst utters short sentences, uses cryptic metaphors, and speaks after long periods of complete silence. Such mesmerizing drama might be good for the practice of hypnosis but is inadvisable for psychoanalysis.

To combat it, the analyst must avoid undue ambiguity and obfuscation. For instance, while recommending analysis, he or she must answer the patient's questions about the frequency of sessions, the recumbent posture, the need for free association, and even the difference between psychotherapy and psychoanalysis in a factual and straightforward manner. Going one step further,

Helmut Thoma suggests that the analyst should share with the patient, from time to time, his or her reasons for making a particular intervention during the course of their work. Such 'demystification' prevents analysis from becoming an idealized and exotic form of mind reading.

71

Imaginary interlocutors

At times, using an imaginary person's voice to make an interpretation turns out to be a remarkably effective device. For instance, the analyst might say 'what might an older brother, had you had one, say in response to this?' Such interpretation can also be made in a reverse form. To an analysand displaying much shyness about his desires for love in paternal transference, the analyst might respond by saying 'what would you say to me if you were a very loving father of mine?' Delivered in either form, such interventions make vivid the object relational scenarios lying dormant in the patient's inner world besides breathing life into the molasses of the daily clinical dialogue.

72

When not to give the bill to a patient?

Some analysts give their monthly bill to the patient at the beginning of a session while others do so at the end of the session. Each practice has its pros and cons. The former can derail what might have been the patient's spontaneous associations but provides an opportunity to instill a modicum of 'reality' in the relationship about which the patient has ample time to talk, if he or she wishes. The latter keeps the unfolding of the session pristine but creates the potential of denying any feelings about receiving a bill from one's analyst. Clearly, one way of doing things is not necessarily better than the other, though maintaining consistency in the ritual does help reduce some of its murkiness. One thing is, however, certain. The analyst (especially if he or she typically gives the bill at the beginning of a session) must not hand the patient a bill in the very first session after a longish break (due to vacations, illness etc.). This conveys a self-centered sense of priorities, comes across as lacking compassion, can foreclose patient's associations, and is simply ill-mannered.

73

Humility

Humility before the breakthrough of arrogance is a clever defense. Humility after such a slip-up is undoing by contrition. Humility in the absence of arrogance is a virtue. The analysts who possess this virtue recognize that they cannot treat certain kinds of patients, seek peer consultation in difficult situations, and stop taking analytic cases upon reaching a certain age.

74

Which form of racism is worse?

Two types of racist remarks appear in the clinical discourse. One is the patient's use of racist tropes (and even epithets) directed at the analyst while in the throes of negative transference. The other is the patient's *en passant* derision of ethno-racial minorities with no particular reference to the analyst and a smug indifference to the hostile nature of such comments. Of note here is the paradox that while the first stings more, it is the second which is more malignant and poses greater clinical challenges.

75

Masochistic funnel

Self-pity exerts a magnetic pull on any and all travails of daily life. Thus a bout of common cold, a gurgling noise emanating from the engine of one's car, or an inability to connect with one's girlfriend because she is out shopping and has turned her cell phone off, can all be enlisted as yet another source of injustice in life. Passing through a masochistic funnel, such events result in thoughts like: 'first I was neglected as a child and now my car is conking out' or 'when I was four my mother died and now I can't reach my girlfriend on the phone,' and so on. Interventions aimed to de-link such unrelated events clog the masochistic funnel and facilitate the analysis of the unconscious pleasure in this self-induced suffering.

76

The novelist and the poet

A novelist and a poet reside within the psychoanalyst. Sometimes they 'come out' and lead the analyst to write and publish actual novels and poetry. More often, they struggle inwardly with each other. The novelist listens to the content, notes its twists and turns, and tries to put two plus two together. The poet listens not to words but to their music, hums under his breath, and gathers seedless echoes of history. The novelist pushes for a coherent narrative, even if it is temporally disjointed on the surface and involves too many flashbacks. The poet eschews order and is content with surprising and almost traumatizing emergence of fresh metaphors. Both the novelist and the poet find 'explanations' for the material being offered to the analyst but in different ways and at different levels of abstraction.

77

Analyst's boredom

Psychoanalysts feel bored when they are unable to use their analytic work egos. This can result from preoccupied states of their own, total identification with a disinterested parent of the patient, an envious assault on their reflective function by the patient, and the intractable 'shallowness' of a patient's mind.

78

Analyst's financial status

Technical challenges in the treatment of both indigent and phenomenally wealthy patients constitute the topic of many psychoanalytic papers and book chapters. Little attention has, however, been paid to the wrinkles added to the therapeutic process due to the analyst being financially compromised or truly wealthy.

79

Where does the analyst look?

When patients with repressed exhibitionism begin lying on the couch, they desperately want to know what the analyst, out of their sight and sitting behind them, is looking at. What they do not realize is that the function of looking loses its value (becomes 'decathected,' in psychoanalytic terms) and the analyst's attention is directed at listening to what the patient is saying and at the inner goings-on of his or her own mind. The analyst is not looking at anything at all. In fact, if the analyst finds himself or herself pointedly gazing at something or observing the patient's posture or movements on the couch intently, it is a sign that some departure—however subtle—from the usual discourse within the dyad has occurred. Now, this is something that, with due apologies for the pun, really needs looking into.

80

Insight addiction

Some patients, unless challenged, will stay in analysis forever. Each day they claim that more needs to be explored and understood about their inhibitions, symptoms, and anxieties, even though years and years have gone by in which pretty much every grain of their mental life has passed through the analytic sieve.

Faced with such insistence, analysts tend to go on 'analyzing'; this trajectory is smoothened if the patient seems psychologically minded, is attractive in some other way as well, and pays a handsome fee. What gets overlooked is the patient's cowardice in leading an autonomous life and his or her view of psychoanalysis as a panacea to all the inherent and inevitable challenges of adult life. Confrontation and interpretation of these themes is essential to resolve what George Awad termed the patient's 'insight addiction.' The process is not painless.

81

Three different outcomes

If things go well, a Freudian analysis leads to mature conventionality, restraint, and thoughtfulness, a Kleinian analysis to enhanced gratitude, self-criticism, and humility, and a Winnicottian analysis to greater authenticity, vitality, and playfulness. If things do not go well, a Freudian analysis produces a caricature of normalcy which erodes with the passage of time, a Kleinian analysis to false modesty which conceals scornful moral superiority, and a Winnicottian analysis to audacity masquerading as straightforwardness.

82

Why not this at the end?

Most case reports demonstrating the successful outcome of an analysis end on the familiar notes of 'by this time, the patient was involved in a deeply satisfying romantic relationship' or 'the patient had finally obtained the promotion he always wanted' or 'the patient decided to quit his firm where he had felt undervalued and chronically mistreated,' and so on.

Tongue-in-cheek though it might sound, a question can be raised as to why no analysis ends on the following notes: 'the patient went to the Dean of his medical school and asked for a pay reduction saying that the widespread poverty in the world made his high salary unconscionable' or 'the patient concluded that he had read too many books in his life and most for wrong reasons. As a result, he decided he will never read another book and will devote his evenings to watching game shows on tv' or 'this elderly and childless widow decided that she would sell her house, give away most of her money to combat sex trafficking of minors, and spend the rest of her days smoking pot in a studio apartment.'

83

The fate of the analyst's bills

Some patients diligently save each monthly bill they receive from their analysts. The stack accumulated over years can turn into a transitional object, a fecal penis, a concrete defense against letting go of the analyst, and a reassuring token of having given as much as one took from the analyst. A gentle inquiry about the fate of one's bills towards termination is therefore a part of good analytic technique.

84

Uttering an adult patient's first name

In an ongoing clinical hour with an adult patient, only two indications exist that necessitate the analyst's using his or her first name. One is when the analyst is describing a reconstructed scenario or mirroring one that the patient has just recounted; 'I can see little Bob (or Julie) looking out of the window and crying as Daddy drives off in his car.' A second indication, suggested by Vamık Volkan, is during an episode of emotional flooding. Including the patient's name in labeling the overwhelming affect (e.g., 'John, you are very very angry right now') humanizes the patient, rekindles the myriad situations of diverse affective hues in which the patient has heard his name spoken, and subtly conveys that the analyst has not become confused by what seems like a core transformation of his identity during a profound emotional turmoil.

85

Procrastination and nail-biting

While many character traits (e.g., being in a hurry, fear of public speaking, inability to accept compliments) loosen their grip on daily behavior as a consequence of analysis, other 'habits' seem too deeply entrenched to be relinquished. Procrastination and nail-biting, for instance, do not go away following analytic treatment.

86

Stillness

With some patients and at selected moments with most patients, the analyst needs to avoid the slightest of postural shift or other bodily movement. By remaining totally immobile, the analyst turns into an ideal, if nearly inanimate, 'container' into which the patient can pour his or her inner turmoil.

87

Cats, not dogs

In conducting treatment via Skype (or any other video format), one often encounters the patient's pets on the screen. While this can have many meanings, it is often the patient's way of triangulating the relationship with the therapist and/or seeking unadulterated admiration and love for their own infantile part that is securely deposited in the pet. The 'intrusion' sometimes happens spontaneously with the pet inserting itself into the clinical space. At other times, it is the patient who cajoles the animal to join the dialogue.

Regardless of how they come about, the striking thing about such moments is that they involve cats far more frequently than dogs. The reasons for this are unclear but three possibilities include: (a) cats are less bulky, less noisy, and less intrusive than dogs so they are not locked out of the room where the patient is calling from, (b) cats are more narcissistic than dogs, more threatened by their owners' attention to someone else, and therefore want to grab a piece of action, and (c) cat owners are certain of their love for their pets but a little uncertain of their pets' love for them (as opposed to dog owners who feel loved beyond any doubt by their pets) and as a consequence need to display their pet, letting the therapist know that they have other sources and objects of love as well.

88

Countertransference sublimation

During clinical sessions, the analyst experiences, bears, and learns from his own subjective processes. A white gamut of associations, memories, fantasies, impulses, and affects are mobilized in his mind. Ideally, such 'countertransference' is subjected by the analyst to analytic scrutiny and the resulting knowledge is utilized for therapeutic purposes. However, when things go awry, enactments, blind spots, and boundary violations occur. These extremes are well covered in psychoanalytic literature. What remains unaddressed is a third possibility and that is of 'countertransference sublimation' whereby the analyst channels his feelings about a patient towards a socially productive act (e.g., writing a book, teaching, helping others in difficulty, and even a bit of social activism).

89

Financial extremes

Both phenomenal wealth and extreme poverty are adversaries of psychoanalysis. The former allows a narcissistic restructuring of reality that can lead to disinterest in deeper intrapsychic life. The latter pulls attention away from the internal world for exactly the opposite reason; problems in external reality become too preoccupying and consuming. One tempts the patient to find exciting and esoteric solutions (e.g., luxurious spas, exotic retreats, renowned gurus) for emotional difficulties, the other renders the four- to five-times-a-week treatment required by psychoanalysis out of reach. In the end, psychoanalysis turns out to be a treatment largely for the upper middle class. This sad reality needs to be faced by the profession.

90

The analyst's dog

There are many actual and apocryphal tales associated with Freud's chows, Jofi, Lun, and Wolf. And there are quite a few interesting stories—some rather hilarious—about other analysts' dogs as well. Besides, there are reasons for the dog's honorific of being 'man's best friend.' That all this would catch the attention of analysts is hardly surprising.

Indeed many analysts, especially Philip Escoll, Stefano Bolognini, and Christie Platt, have written very good papers about the man–dog relationship and of course there are several others who have addressed the nuances of dog phobia. However, a paper specifically devoted to the analyst's dog and titled as such still waits to be written.

Part IV

Profession

'The child whose home fails to give a feeling of security looks outside his home for the four walls; he still has hope, and looks to grandparents, uncles and aunts, friends of the family, school (for) an external stability without which he may go mad.'

Donald Winnicott (1896–1971)

91

The second beard

While Freud's sporting a beard throughout his adult life has made a 'bearded Freudian' the staple of print media cartoons, the fact is that all his early followers including Jung, Adler, Ferenczi, Abraham, Rank, Sachs, Eitingon, and Jones were clean-shaven. The same is true of the subsequent generations of great analysts including Fairbairn, Winnicott, Balint, Bion, Sandler, Britton, Casement, and Parsons in England; Lacan, Green, and Anzieu in France; Bolognini in Italy; and Erikson, Sullivan, Stone, Searles, Arlow, Brenner, Kohut, Kernberg, Blum, and Mitchell in the United States. In all honesty though, it should be acknowledged that Ernest Jones did grow a beard in the final years of his life when Freud had passed away.

92

Psychiatry and psychoanalysis

In many regions of the psychoanalytic world, psychiatry and psychoanalysis did not develop close links. In the United States they were married to each other for a long time. This union has fallen apart and now they are all but divorced.

Both parties contributed to this rupture. *Psychoanalysts*, filling most chairmanships and senior academic positions from the 1950s to the early 1980s, exploited the system by 'double-dipping' in the form of earning money by private practice during hours paid by their medical school jobs. They spoke and wrote in a language that was not understood by their non-psychoanalyst colleagues. Worse, they regarded the latter as second-class citizens of the mental health community and looked at them with barely veiled contempt. All this sowed seeds of professional strife. *Psychiatrists*, ascending to powerful positions in the post-Watergate era and buoyed by the emerging DSM movement, took swift revenge. Assisted by insurance companies' zeal for accountability and the alluring promise of new psychopharmacology, they banished psychoanalysts and their vaguely threatening ideas from professional nomenclature. The shameless lack of interest in depth psychology among some of these psychiatrists imparted a messianic flavor to their sadism. The ground for bloodshed was set.

93

Do we need a prefix to 'psychoanalysis'?

Following Ferenczi's egalitarian 'Mutual Psychoanalysis' and Rosen's confrontational 'Direct Psychoanalysis,' a spate of approaches implying radical differences with 'Classical Psychoanalysis' have popped up. Prominent among these are 'Interpersonal Psychoanalysis' (Sullivan), 'Modern Psychoanalysis' (Spotnitz), 'Relational Psychoanalysis' (Mitchell), 'Practical Psychoanalysis' (Renik), 'Essential Psychoanalysis' (Sripada), 'Quantum Psychoanalysis' (Gargiulo), and so on. The question is whether this denotational zeal reflects a sublimated aspiration for further specialization within a discipline or is the relentless rebranding of itself as a form of resistance to psychoanalysis? What mobilizes the creation of these labels? A well-earned pride over innovation or weak-kneed surrender to hubris?

94

Jewish psychoanalysis, Christian psychoanalysis

It might be 'politically incorrect' to comment upon it, but the fact is that there exists a 'Jewish psychoanalysis' and a 'Christian psychoanalysis.' The former (represented by Freud, Klein, and Anna Freud) seems anchored in skepticism, stoic ethics, doubt about basic human goodness, respect for speaking, and interpretive interventions. The latter (represented by Fairbairn, Winnicott, and Guntrip) seems anchored in credulousness, romantic ethics, doubt about basic human badness, respect for silence, and affirmative interventions. One relies upon the 'survival of the subject,' the other on the 'survival of the object.' The first (Jewish psychoanalysis) reflects the mentality of a persecuted minority while the second (Christian psychoanalysis) reflects the mentality of a dominant majority.

95

Pauses

Pauses that interrupt patients' flow of speech can be categorized into four types: (1) pauses that come after a conjunction like 'and,' 'or,' 'but' (e.g., 'I am thinking of moving to New York and …' and at this point the patient falls silent), (2) pauses that function like a comma (e.g., 'Sometimes I want to commit suicide'; the patient stops and then adds 'Not really'), (3) pauses that reflect genuine blankness and leave the patients themselves confused (e.g., 'I am studying very hard for this course … Oh! what was saying?'), and (4) pauses that seem dramatic and assure that the listener remains attentive (e.g., 'Just my sister raised her voice, my father …' and the patient falls silent). These four types of pause require different ways of responding. Respectively, such interventions include (1) inquiring about what was to follow the pause, (2) ignoring the post-pause phrase and focusing on the pre-pause segment of the sentence, (3) inviting the patient to fantasize about where or to whom he or she might have gone to meet during the blank period, and (4) linking the 'hook' aspect of the pause to other consciously expressed concerns that others might lose interest in one's narrative and, even, one's existence at large.

96

Writers and non-writers

The writer and the 'non-writer' differ in two important ways. The writer is arrogant and hard working. He considers his private thoughts to be important and is willing to put in the effort to make them public. The non-writer dismisses his thoughts as unimportant and avoids the work required to put them into a written form. He is honorably humble but lazy.

97

Analysts' memoirs

The term 'personal myth' was coined by Ernst Kris for the defensive, palatable, and mostly self-serving narrative an individual evolves about his or her life. Undergoing psychoanalysis puts such assemblage into question and, at times, changes it considerably. Memoirs written by analysts are valiant, if desperate, efforts at restoring their 'personal myths.' What is told, which pieces the stories emphasize, what is left out, which characters are depicted favorably, who is given short shrift, and what motivations are assigned to others and even to the earlier versions of one's own self are all tricks of a magician disguised as a writer. To put it bluntly the enterprise is nothing but a Russian-doll syndrome.

98

Was Bion Hindu?

Wilfred Bion's recommendation for the analyst to be free of all 'memory and desire' in encountering his patient bears a striking resemblance to the detached perceptualism expounded by the great Hindu philosopher Jiddu Krishnamurthi. The latter, for instance, is known to have said that if one holds in one's hand a little animal with feathers, two wings, a beak, and the capacity to fly, one can only see the animal till the moment the word 'bird' has entered the mind. At this point, one stops seeing the animal.

A predominantly Hindu nation, even if under British control at the time, India was where Bion was born, raised, abruptly removed from, and the 'motherland' to which he never returned. Two of his major concepts embody this poignant saga: (a) 'attacks on linking,' which enshrines his brutal separation from his beloved Hindu nanny, and (b) 'O' which echoes 'Om' (signifying the Absolute Essence of God), the chant he heard in the visits he regularly made to Hindu temples in the company of his nanny. The fact that Bion's childhood nanny often referred to him as 'my little Krishna' adds further spice to the Hindu hypothesis delineated here.

99

PEP vetting

Admittedly an odd phrase, especially in its phonetic kinship with bed-wetting, PEP vetting refers to psychoanalytic writers cross-checking the bibliographies of their papers with the existing citations on PEP-Web (an electronic compendium of psychoanalytic literature spanning over 125 years and containing the full contents of over 139,000 published papers). Doing so would (a) preclude offering preexisting notions as original, (b) pay due respect to earlier contributors to the subject, and (c) challenge the author to situate his or her work in the context of evolving thought on the matter under consideration. In light of such benefits to scholarship, it is surprising that no psychoanalytic journal has made PEP vetting a requirement for papers submitted to it for publication.

100

Age-specific writing

Some papers and books can only be written when the psychoanalyst has reached an old age. In part this has to do with the breadth of vision that long-term experience provides and in part is due to the freedom from organizational concerns one acquires with seniority. It then becomes less important how one's peers and the local or national professional association would react to the ideas being proposed than the need or desire to express them. Works that contain delicate self disclosures, botched sessions, political and religious convictions, and much professional 'spleen and nostalgia'—incidentally, the title of John Gedo's memoir—are best published in one's late seventies or eighties. To wit, the book in your hands itself belongs to the sort of writing mentioned here.

101

The 'domestication' of analysis

Some analysts take pride in keeping their analytic listening 'on' all the time. They listen to what their spouses, children, and other family members or friends say 'like an analyst' and do not hesitate to respond accordingly. This is a travesty of a true psychoanalytic attitude which respects the ethics of consent, collaboration, and care. The fact that most 'interpretive' remarks made by such analysts unmask 'badness' in others testifies to their sadistic intent. Such misuse of psychoanalysis is akin to a surgeon's use of a scalpel for peeling potatoes.

102

Childless child analysts

Not only did the great child analysts like Anna Freud, Margaret Mahler, and Donald Winnicott not have children of their own, Hermine Hug-Hellmuth, the founder of child analysis, was also childless. The potential impact of childlessness upon the theories and technical approaches of these four child analysts has, however, not been explored.

103

Three tips for supervisors

A supervisory frame is strengthened by (a) the two parties sharing some factual information about themselves (e.g., age, marital status, children, educational background, major formative influences, talents) with each other; this does not eradicate the development of mutual transferences but does diminish their intensity and keeps the relationship better grounded in reality, (b) making sure that the identity of the supervisee's analyst remains unknown to the supervisor; this frees him or her to speak about matters of technique without worrying about how the candidate's analyst works, and (c) seeing some photographs (including that of the couch–chair placement) of the supervisee's office; this makes their interaction more vivid and ecologically anchored for the supervisor, hence deepens his or her capacity to be of use to the supervisee.

104

Non-analyst friends

A psychoanalyst draws great benefit from his friendship with individuals who do not belong to the mental health field but are, say, economists, lawyers, engineers, businessmen, investment bankers, or political scientists. Not only do such people teach the analyst that human choices are governed by non-psychological factors as well, they keep him 'civilized' by displaying appropriate horror when, during the course of a lovely dinner, he begins talking about the sadistic glee in cutting off the head of an annoying sibling, the dread of being castrated by the father, and the joyous intrigue of maternal orgasm!

105

The future of psychoanalysis

The question 'What is the future of psychoanalysis?' is simply too broad to be answered in a meaningful way. Slicing the inquiry into the following categories paves the way for a serious response: (a) future in which region of the world, (b) future in medicine or outside of it, (c) future in its mainstream form or in modified versions, and (d) future with the fees currently being charged or at much lesser rates? Such fine-tuning of inquiry is more likely to yield useful responses than merely asking 'What is the future of psychoanalysis?'

106

Blood killing

North American psychoanalysis, with a few of its training centers being shining exceptions, has turned into a nine-year-old girl with a hemoglobin level of five. The tragic nature of the situation is compounded by the girl's mother begging for an immediate blood transfusion without any testing of its match and safety while the girl's father, a Jehovah's Witness, refuses to let her receive any blood at all. Both parents feel virtuous. Both are putting their child's life at risk.

107

Un-associated and un-affiliated

A prominent analyst, who had gained considerable prominence in a different realm under a pseudonym, told me that he keeps his two careers totally 'un-associated.' I was taken aback by it, did not know what to make of such a psychic split, could not grasp how that was even possible, since the analyst's other career involved words, fables, and long-forgotten myths.

Another well-known analyst was introduced to me by a colleague with flowery remarks that glorified the 'famous guy' not being a member of any psychoanalytic organization, be it local, regional, national, or international. I was puzzled and failed to figure out what was praiseworthy about such a solipsism.

Both encounters left me a bit unnerved. I don't know about you, but I like my analysts to be better integrated, inside and out!

108

Analysts turned gurus

Some analysts who are much admired by others begin to admire themselves very much. Such narcissistic inflation leads them to become 'gurus.' Among the early symptoms of this slippage are their (a) resigning from major professional organizations, (b) becoming hyper-inventive in language and coining new words and phrases, (c) stopping publishing in peer-reviewed forums, (d) accruing a fiercely loyal group of fans, and (e) at times, moving to another city and changing their vestimental preferences.

109

Taboos

While clinical and organizational discourse in psychoanalysis has recently become more open, tabooed topics still exist. Many analysts fear speaking openly in professional settings and are overly cautious in their writing. Dread of being maligned and ostracized propels them to secrecy; this is not good for the growth and advancement of the field.

110

The analyst's funeral

At their funerals, most psychoanalysts are declared to have been humble people (while many of them were not) and sent away to the blessed arms of God (in whom most of them did not believe). The first practice taxes the credulity of the participants. The second invalidates the truth of the deceased. Mendacity puts on the tuxedo of sanctimony and the somber nature of the occasion permits the masquerade to go unquestioned.

111

Alternate pathways

Helping one's patients, reading a good book, going for a walk, eating some really good ice cream, playing with a dog, and making love with one's partner seem far better ways of spending one's days and nights than ruminating about the bygone beauty of the early psychoanalytic movement and arguing about the baroque bureaucracy and burdensome bylaws of psychoanalytic organizations.

Acknowledgments

Like Freud said of dreams, ideas for a book also come 'from above' and 'from below.' The former refers to triggers in external reality and the latter to preexisting emotional issues. My reasons for writing this book 'from above' include my encounters with three recent books: Patrick Casement's *Credo?* (2020), Brett Kahr's *How to Flourish as a Psychotherapist* (2020), and Andrea Celenza's *Transference, Love, Being* (2023). The precise and elegant expression of these authors touched me deeply and reignited my long-lasting admiration of the writings of the great Argentinian poet Jorge Luis Borges and late philosopher-psychoanalyst, Allen Wheelis. This brings me to the reasons for writing this book that came 'from below.' These include my daughter, Nishat, explaining to me the difference between 'receiving' and 'taking' when, during a crisis, I was hesitant to accept her help, and also from my sense that, getting old now, I might not have time left to develop all the ideas floating in my mind into fully developed papers.

My beloved muse and life-partner, Müge Alkan, not only listened to these pieces almost immediately after I wrote them at all hours of days and nights but also prepared the manuscript of this book for publication. Others who lent me their ears include Drs Aisha Abbasi, Ira Brenner, Ann Eichen, Rajnish Mago, Christie Platt, J. Anderson Thomson, Jr, and Thomas Wolman. Ms Caroline Culverhouse, a graduate of the psychotherapy training program of the Psychoanalytic Center of Philadelphia, also helped in subtle ways. To all these individuals, my sincere thanks indeed.

About the author

Salman Akhtar is Professor of Psychiatry at Jefferson Medical College and a Training and Supervising Analyst at the Psychoanalytic Center of Philadelphia. A prolific contributor to psychoanalytic literature, Dr Akhtar has published 108 books of which twenty-three are solo-authored. Prominent among these are *Broken Structures* (1992), *Immigration and Identity* (1999), *Comprehensive Dictionary of Psychoanalysis* (2009), *Tales of Transformation* (2022), and *In Leaps and Bounds* (2022). He has delivered plenary addresses at the conferences of both the American Psychoanalytic and the International Psychoanalytic Associations. He has served on the editorial boards of the *International Journal of Psychoanalysis*, the *Journal of the American Psychoanalytic Association*, and *Psychoanalytic Quarterly* and received many honors including the highly prestigious Sigourney Award (2012) for Distinguished Contributions to Psychoanalysis. Dr Akhtar is also a poet and has eighteen collections of poetry to his credit.

Name index

Abraham, Karl, 117
Adler, Alfred, 117
Akhtar, Salman, 11
Anzieu, Didier, 117
Arlow, Jacob, 117
Awad, George, 102

Balint, Enid, 81
Balint, Michael, 117
Bateson, Gregory, 46
Benedek, Therese, 16
Bion, Wilfred, 117, 126–127
Bleuler, Eugen, 21
Bleuler, Manfred, 21
Blum, Harold, 117
Bolognini, Stefano, 114, 117

Brenner, Ira, 117
Britton, Ronald, 117

Carpelan, Henrik, 11
Casement, Patrick, 117

Eitingon, Max, 117
Erikson, Erik, 117
Escoll, Philip, 114

Fairbairn, Ronald., 117, 121
Ferenczi, Sándor, 5, 18, 71, 84, 117, 120
Freud, Anna, 74, 121, 131
Freud, Sigmund, 2, 3, 12, 25, 30, 34, 38, 56, 57, 64, 72, 74, 79, 114, 117, 121

NAME INDEX

Gargiulo, Gerald, 120
Gerald, Mark, 11
Green, André, 35, 117
Guntrip, Harry, 121

Hug-Hellmuth, Hermine, 131

Jones, Ernest, 117
Jung, Carl Gustav, 117

Kaczynski, Ted, 45
Kernberg, Otto, 84, 117
Klein, Melanie, 62, 71, 121
Kohut, Heinz, 117
Kris, Ernst, 125
Krishnamurthi, Jiddu, 126
Kundera, Milan, 36

Lacan, Jacques, 117

Mahler, Margaret, 131
Messler Davies, Jody, 5
Mills, Jon, 11
Mitchell, Stephen, 117, 120

Parsons, Michael, 117
Platt, Christie, 114

Rank, Otto, 117
Renik, Owen, 120
Rosen, John, 120

Sachs, Hanns, 117
Sandler, Joseph, 117
Schlesinger, Herbert, 73
Searles, Harold, 117
Sharpe, Ella Freeman, 84
Spotnitz, Hyman, 120
Sripada, Bhaskar, 120
Stone, Leo, 117
Sullivan, Harry Stack, 117, 120

Thoma, Helmut, 91

Unabomer *see* Kaczynski, Ted

Van der Kolk, Bessel, 5
Volkan, Vamık, 41, 107

Winnicott, Donald, 12–13, 116, 117, 121, 131